ROCKS

By Rowena Mouda

Library For All Ltd.

Rocks

First published 2023

Published by Library For All Ltd
Email: info@libraryforall.org
URL: libraryforall.org

Our Yarning logo design by Jason Lee, Bidjipidji Art

Original illustrations by Natia Warda

Rocks
Mouda, Rowena
ISBN: 978-1-923063-05-1
SKU03391

ROCKS

Rocks can be heavy,
and they can be light.

Rocks can be smooth, and they can be rough.

Rocks can be big, and they can be small.

Rocks can be many different colours.

Rocks can be in rivers,
and they can be
in oceans.

Rocks can be in
the desert,

and they can be on mountains.

Rocks can be toys on Country and near water.

Rocks can be useful
to us in many ways.

Rocks are special
to me.

You can use these questions to talk about this book with your family, friends and teachers.

What did you learn from this book?

Describe this book in one word. Funny? Scary? Colourful? Interesting?

How did this book make you feel when you finished reading it?

What was your favourite part of this book?

download our reader app
getlibraryforall.org

About the author

Rowena was born in Derby from the Dari, Oomeday, Yowjabai and Nyikina groups. She loves sharing stories, fishing and being with family. Rowena's favourite stories are her grandmother's family stories about when she was young.

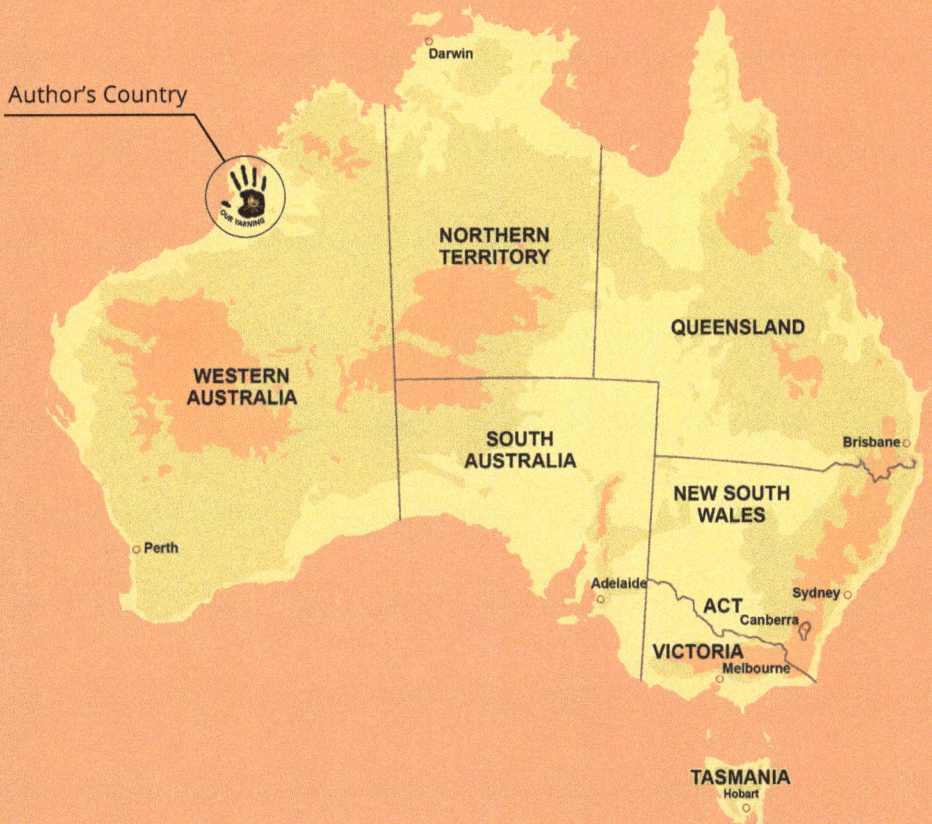

Author's Country

Darwin

NORTHERN
TERRITORY

QUEENSLAND

WESTERN
AUSTRALIA

SOUTH
AUSTRALIA

NEW SOUTH
WALES

Brisbane

Perth

Adelaide

Sydney

ACT
Canberra

VICTORIA
Melbourne

TASMANIA
Hobart

Our Yarning

Want to discover more books from this collection? Our Yarning is a collection of books written by Aboriginal and Torres Strait Islander peoples across Australia.

We know that children learn better, and enjoy reading more, when they see themselves in the stories, characters and illustrations of the books they read.

To download the app, visit the Google Play Store on any Android device and search 'Our Yarning'.

libraryforall.org